Granny at the Park

by **Damian Harvey** and **Jan Smith**

"I like the park,"

said Granny.

3

"I like the swings,"

said Granny.

"I like the slide,"

said Granny.

"I like the horse,"

said Granny.

9

"I like the roundabout,"

said Granny.

"I like the shop,"

said Granny.

"I like the pond,"

said Granny.

"I like the ducks,"

said Granny.

"I like the park,"

said Granny.

Story trail

Start at the beginning of the story trail. Ask your child to retell the story in their own words, pointing to each picture in turn to recall the sequence of events.

Start

Independent Reading

This series is designed to provide an opportunity for your child to read on their own. These notes are written for you to help your child choose a book and to read it independently.

In school, your child's teacher will often be using reading books which have been banded to support the process of learning to read. Use the book band colour your child is reading in school to help you make a good choice. *Granny at the Park* is a good choice for children reading at Pink 1b in their classroom to read independently.

The aim of independent reading is to read this book with ease, so that your child enjoys the story and relates it to their own experiences.

About the book

In this story, Granny pays a visit to the park with her grandson. She ends up going on everything in the playground and even gets the biggest ice cream. Her grandson is not impressed!

Before reading

Help your child to learn how to make good choices by asking: "Why did you choose this book? Why do you think you will enjoy it?" Support your child to think about what they already know about the story context. Look at the cover together and ask: "What do you think the story will be about?" Read the title aloud and ask: "Who do you think will go on the swing? And what about the slide?" Remind your child that they can try to sound out the letters to make a word if they get stuck.

Decide together whether your child will read the story independently or read it aloud to you. When books are short, as at Pink 1b, your child may wish to do both!

During reading

If reading aloud, support your child if they hesitate or ask for help by telling the word. Remind your child of what they know and what they can do independently.

If reading to themselves, remind your child that they can come and ask for your help if stuck.

After reading

Support comprehension by asking your child to tell you about the story. Help your child think about the messages in the book that go beyond the story and ask: "Do you think the boy liked going to the park with Granny? Who do you think had the better time at the park, Granny or the boy? Why do you think that?"

Give your child a chance to respond to the story: "Did you have a favourite part? What do you like most about visiting the park?"

Use the story trail to encourage your child to retell the story in the right sequence, in their own words.

Extending learning

Help your child extend the story structure by using the same sentence pattern and changing the context. "Where else could Granny visit? Let's change the story so Granny goes somewhere else. What might she get up to? Let's imagine she went to the beach. 'I like the beach,' said Granny. Now you think of what she might like at the beach. She might jump in the waves: 'I like the waves,' said Granny."

On a few of the pages, check your child can finger point accurately by asking them to show you how they kept their place in the print by tracking from word to word.

Help your child to use letter information by asking them to find the interest word on each page by using the first letter. For example: "Which word is 'pond'? How do you know it is that word?"

Franklin Watts
First published in Great Britain in 2017
by The Watts Publishing Group

Copyright © The Watts Publishing Group 2017

Series Editors: Jackie Hamley and Melanie Palmer
Series Advisors: Dr Sue Bodman and Glen Franklin
Series Designer: Peter Scoulding

A CIP catalogue record for this book is
available from the British Library.

ISBN 978 1 4451 5419 0 (hbk)
ISBN 978 1 4451 5420 6 (pbk)

Printed in China

Franklin Watts
An imprint of
Hachette Children's Group
Part of The Watts Publishing Group
Carmelite House
50 Victoria Embankment
London EC4Y 0DZ

An Hachette UK Company
www.hachette.co.uk

www.franklinwatts.co.uk

FSC
www.fsc.org
MIX
Paper from
responsible sources
FSC® C104740